For a believer who takes the gospel seriously, the death of an unbeliever can be one of the most desperately traumatic experiences in life. We struggle to know how to react, to grieve, and to come to terms with such deep sorrow. Will Dobbie has done us a great service in this deeply biblical and theological book. His theology is robustly reformed, his heart is warmly pastoral, and his counsel is wonderfully God-centered and realistic. I warmly commend this most helpful book.

CHRISTOPHER ASH
Writer-in-Residence, Tyndale House, Cambridge;
Author, *Bible Delight*

Burying a loved one when you are uncertain of their eternal destiny forces us to wrestle with God in ways we had not anticipated. We can be left disoriented and despairing. *A Time to Mourn* is a remarkable resource that helps our anxious hearts find peace in the God whose ways are above ours. No book can heal a broken heart, but this work draws you face to face with the One who can.

J. GARRETT KELL
Pastor, Del Ray Baptist Church, Alexandria, Virginia;
Author, *Church: Do I Have To Go?*

Everyone experiences the loss of a loved one at some point in their lives and when they do, they will need the consolation of the gospel and their heavenly Father's tender care of his children. In *A Time to Mourn*, Will Dobbie has provided us with a beautiful condensation of what we can know about our Father's tender care. Knowing God in this way will prove a balm in the midst of sorrow and strength in the face of debilitating weakness. Thoroughly recommended.

DEREK W. H. THOMAS
Senior Minister, First Presbyterian Church, Columbia, South Carolina;
Teaching Fellow, Ligonier Ministries

T0015668

Will Dobbie has done Christians a great service in writing *A Time To Mourn*. In the book he tackles the painful and often unaddressed topic of the death of unbelieving loved ones. The seven short chapters are written with doctrinal precision, pastoral sensitivity and practical wisdom. What makes this work most outstanding, however, is its God-centeredness. People who know the character of their sovereign, gracious God are best equipped to deal with suffering. This book is a gem.

GAVIN PEACOCK
Former professional footballer; Pastor,
Author, *A Greater Glory: From Pitch to Pulpit*

We all need this book! And we all need the pastor's heart behind it, to comfort us in the painful uncertainty of losing unbelieving loved ones. Will Dobbie doesn't reassure us with empty sentiments or cliché verses, but with the very character of our good God Himself. In this sorrow, there is no better anchor.

NATALIE BRAND
Bible teacher;
Author, *Prone to Wander: Grace for the Lukewarm and Apathetic*

Every one of us will find ourselves indebted to Will Dobbie for this beautiful book, because every one of us will find ourselves in the valley of the shadow of death. He leads us to God, not a passive God, but One who is engaged with His people in all their afflictions; a God whose attributes bring comfort and strength to the weak and weary saint. I commend it warmly and am grateful to its author for pointing me again to the Author of all things.

LIAM GOLIGHER
Pastor, Tenth Presbyterian Church, Philadelphia, Pennsylvania

Have you ever found yourself speechless as you attempt to comfort the loved ones of a person who entered eternity outside Christ? You are not alone. In *A Time to Mourn*, Will Dobbie has broken the silence on a difficult (and almost taboo) subject with pastoral compassion, realism, and biblical faithfulness. His treatment is profoundly experiential, applicatory, and engaging (his selection of illustrations from Scripture, church history, culture, and his own life are splendid). Above all, Dobbie locates his treatment firmly in the character of God, including His care, sympathy, omniscience, and justice. A valuable contribution to both poimenics and practical Christian literature!

JOEL R. BEEKE
Chancellor, Puritan Reformed Theological Seminary, Grand Rapids, Michigan; Author, *Knowing and Growing in Assurance of Faith*

I thank God for Will Dobbie's soldier's courage. It has meant that when confronted with the horror of the death of loved ones, who have rejected Christ, he has not shied away, but forced himself to engage biblically and pastorally with this grievous subject. The result is a book on God's character that I wish I had read 30 years ago at the start of my ministry.

RICO TICE
Evangelist;
Co-Founder of Christianity Explored Ministries

Will Dobbie offers us solace in Jesus in *A Time to Mourn* – an accessible, compassionate, unflinchingly biblical application of the gospel to the heart-wrenching experience of uncertain loss. A must-read for those seeking solace and understanding in the face of profound grief – a reminder that, in Christ, there is comfort for every affliction.

ERIC M. SCHUMACHER
Podcaster; Songwriter;
Author, *Ours: Biblical Comfort for Men Grieving Miscarriages*

When a loved one dies, we grieve the loss. We weep and mourn. As Christians, we find hope in our loved one's eternal destiny and that joy mingles with our sorrow. But what about when a loved one dies outside of Christ? *A Time to Mourn* speaks to this specific kind of grief. Gently and compassionately, Will Dobbie digs into God's Word to speak to this special kind of sorrow. In doing so, he draws us to the comfort that can only be found in our good and sovereign God. *A Time to Mourn* is gospel filled, tender and kind, practical and theological. Anyone who has grieved a loved one that died apart from faith needs to read this book.

CHRISTINA FOX
Counselor; Speaker;
Author, *The Great Big Sad: Finding Comfort in Grief and Loss*

Will Dobbie offers tremendous wisdom and pastoral insight on a topic that many know, but few have dealt with. *A Time to Mourn* will be a helpful companion to those who are grieving or counseling those who are grieving the death of a loved one whose eternal state is unknown. Dobbie's bedside manner brings comfort to the sufferer and gives them confidence in the justice, grace, and mercy of God.

STEPHEN SPINNENWEBER
Pastor, Westminster Presbyterian Church, Jacksonville, Florida

Some topics get spoken of less often. I've never preached a full sermon to comfort those who have lost someone with an uncertain eternity. This is why I'm thankful Will Dobbie has done more than preach that sermon. He's written a faithful, honest, and comforting book I can give others to explain one of the most troubling experiences in the Christian life.

BENJAMIN VRBICEK
Managing Editor, Gospel-Centered Discipleship;
Pastor, Community Evangelical Free Church, Harrisburg, Pennsylvania

In the darkest corners of our churches sit many who feel alone in their misery. Grief at losing a child. Bewilderment at the death of a seemingly unsaved family member. Shock in the aftermath of suicide. Does anyone understand? Can anyone speak into such despair? In the footsteps of his Saviour, Will Dobbie has walked into the darkness to bring light and comfort to all who mourn. This is a wise and gentle book, full of grace and truth – full of Christ, the man of sorrows and shepherd of the downcast. It will be an immense help not just to those who mourn, but those, too, who want to walk with sufferers in their grief.

Jonty Rhodes
Pastor, Christ Church Central, Leeds;
Author, *Reformed Worship*

Sound, sensitive, and scriptural.

Rob Ventura
Pastor, Grace Community Baptist Church, Providence, Rhode Island;
Author, *Expository Outlines and Observations on Romans*

There are precious few good books on the subject of grief, and none that deals so well with this particularly vexed topic of grieving those who – as far as we can tell – died without faith. Will Dobbie has a clear mind and a pastor's heart, and this winning combination has given us a short but necessary book to help us (and to help us be a help to others). Dobbie outlines some difficult truths for us to hear, but necessary ones for us to believe. Yet, he also matches this with a caring and kind heart as we wrestle with one of the most difficult questions of the Christian life.

Adrian Reynolds
Head of National Ministries, Fellowship of Independent Evangelical Churches, UK; Author, *Teaching Ezra: From Text to Message*

We are certain to encounter grief and questions navigating this world. Where can we go for comfort when there doesn't appear to be any answers? With a pastor's heart, Will Dobbie helpfully guides us to rest in God's character in life's most difficult days.

Erik Raymond
Senior Pastor, Redeemer Fellowship Church,
Boston, Massachusetts; Author, *Is Hell for real?*

Grieving the Loss of Those
Whose Eternities Were Uncertain

A TIME
TO MOURN

WILL DOBBIE

CHRISTIAN
FOCUS

To George

who is more of an inspiration
and an encouragement
than he knows.

CONTENTS

Acknowledgements

Emmanuel Church, Knoxville: your constant encouragement is precious to me, as you live out many of the spiritual realities described in the pages ahead. Thank you.

Alexandra Watson, Adrian Reynolds, Derek Thomas, John Stevens, Benjamin Vrbicek, Natalie Brand, Jonty Rhodes, Andy Prime, Jonathan Carswell, Stephen 'Spin' Spinnenweber, Garrett Kell, Willie MacKenzie, Lainey Greer and Steele Wright: I'm deeply grateful for your help and kindness in looking over the manuscript, and for your theological and pastoral wisdom.

Colin Fast at Christian Focus: brother, your guidance and insights have been invaluable.

My wife, Michelle: the blessing which you are to me is beyond words. Your help, encouragement, example, wisdom and selfless service underpin all that I do, including this book. Thank you.

Introduction

We first met when he was posted to my army unit in Germany. I had been homesick and feeling isolated as an outspoken Christian, and he extended generous, patient friendship to me. We ended up going for long runs together and driving around Europe on weekends. He became my best friend. He was a member of the Parachute Regiment, famed for its rough, tough ethos, but we would analyse classical music together on long drives and he would discuss art with me. His humility and humour were deeply attractive.

One weekend, we were staying in a backpackers' hostel in Berlin. As we lay on rickety old beds in the darkness, I shared the gospel with him. He was polite but non-committal. Another weekend, we went to Amsterdam for him to meet my girlfriend and buy an engagement ring for his own. A few months later, I was playing the organ at his wedding in a beautiful country church in England. (He instructed me to play 'There may be trouble ahead' as he and his bride walked up the aisle, to gales of laughter from the congregation.)

Soon afterwards, we found ourselves in a small base in Iraq, isolated out in the wilderness. We were in different units so hardly crossed paths, given the insane busyness of that period. But one evening, shortly before it happened, when the sand and dust had made for yet another achingly beautiful sunset,

I passed him during a run around the base. I put my arm around his shoulders and we had a joyful catch-up.

A few days later, I was commanding the Quick Reaction Force and we were scrambled to respond to an incident. As we left the base, more information came over the net, including zap numbers of casualties. A zap number is the first two initials of a soldier's name followed by the last four digits of his army number and his blood group. I spent the 20-minute journey to the incident racking my brain over those sets of initials, trying to work out who the casualties were. By the time we arrived, I was satisfied and relieved that I didn't know the victims personally. Wrong. A huge roadside bomb had crushed my friend's vehicle's engine block, obliterated his driver, and decapitated him.

In the months that followed, I agonised over the ways I had (and hadn't) witnessed to him. I writhed as I replayed his reactions to my imperfect expressions of the gospel. Now it was too late. A few months after playing the organ at his wedding, I found myself playing a keyboard at his memorial service. The verses of Scripture in the short ceremony were bitter to my taste as I reflected that, as far as the evidence pointed, they didn't apply to him. He had perished.

The Heartbreaking Taboo

The death of someone you care about, whom you don't think was saved, is surely one of the most heartbreaking of circumstances. It can haunt for a lifetime. Yet the eternal loss of unbelievers is something most believers experience several times over. It's also a taboo: the anguish of the bereaved Christian makes talking to others hard. And those others, in turn, find ministering to the believer hard, given the sensitivity of the issue. Someone recently told me that out of hundreds of believers she has interacted with over the years, who have known about the loss of her gospel-rejecting parent, she can think of only two or three who have shared about a similar loss.

No Shame

If you are struggling with the doctrine of hell, there is no shame in that. You are in good company. A friend of mine recalled walking down a garden path to visit a couple whose apparently unbelieving son had just committed suicide. He is as theologically and pastorally astute as anyone I know, a seasoned pastor who has written some good Christian books. He remembers having literally no idea what to say as he approached the front door. I know a publishing editor with great theology and a strong faith who lost her father unexpectedly four years ago. Having prayed for his salvation since she was twelve, she still had no assurance about this. She has wrestled with this issue ever since, trying to write about it but finding herself emotionally unable. Pastor and theologian, John Piper, admitted in an article that he finds the funerals of blatant unbelievers 'way worse than anything.'*

Consider Job. In the aftermath of devastating suffering which included the violent deaths of children whose spiritual status troubled him,† Job cries out, 'I loathe my life ... I will speak in the bitterness of my soul. I will say to God, "Do not condemn me; let me know why you contend against me. Does it seem good to you to oppress, to despise the work of your hands?"'‡ Yet as Job flails in the darkness with this bewildered grief, God ends up rebuking the friends who had been correcting him, and in fact *commending* him: 'My anger burns against you [Eliphaz] and against your two friends, for you have not spoken of me *what is right, as my servant Job has*.'§

---

* John Piper, 'How do you deal with the death of an unsaved loved one', Desiring God, https://www.desiringgod.org/interviews/how-do-you-deal-with-the-death-of-an-unsaved-loved-one. Accessed 2 January, 2023.

† Job 1:5, 18, 19.

‡ Job 10:1–3.

§ Job 42:7.

No Sin

This indicates that not only is there no *shame* if you're struggling to accept God's actions. There's no *sin* either – as long as you're able to keep hold of whatever truth Job had clung to when God said he had 'spoken of me what is right.' What was that? Job had voiced it just previously:

> I know that you can do all things,
> and that no purpose of yours can be thwarted ...
> Therefore I have uttered what I did not understand,
> things too wonderful for me, which I did not know.*

The truth is that we will not always understand! God's purposes and His justification for His actions will sometimes be 'too wonderful' for us. ('Wonderful' here doesn't mean something to be celebrated as delightful. It means something full of wonder because God is acting far beyond our understanding.) As Job admits elsewhere, we observe 'but the outskirts of His ways, and how small a whisper do we hear of Him? But the thunder of His power who can understand?'† God says through Isaiah, 'As the heavens are higher than the earth, so are my ways higher than your ways and my thoughts than your thoughts.'‡ God calls us to trust, humbly, that He is working in ways mysterious to us. Keep sight of this, and the angst you have over God's actions is without sin, just as it was for Job.

Yet the loss of an unbelieving loved one can, of course, make us re-evaluate our theology. How loving and compassionate is God really? Is He a God I'm able to keep following without resentment? What about predestination? What about babies? What about the severely mentally disabled? And if the person

---

* Job 42:2–3.
† Job 26:14.
‡ Isa. 55:9.

I loved is now in hell, how can I have any consolation, any closure, any peace, ever again?*

Truth and Solace
This book brings the Bible to bear on these and other questions. Four times in Scripture, God condemns false prophets for 'healing the wound of His people lightly' and 'saying, "Peace, peace," when there is no peace.'† As a writer, I don't want to face that condemnation. So we will be looking Scripture honestly as well as sensitively, clearly as well as compassionately. Yet I trust you will discover that more clarity leads to *more* comfort, not less. In the words of C. S. Lewis, '... comfort is the one thing you cannot get by looking for it. If you look for truth, you may find comfort in the end: if you look for comfort you will not get either comfort or truth – only ... wishful thinking ... and, in the end, despair.'‡

May you experience truth and perhaps unexpected comfort and solace in the pages ahead.

---

* Another question might be 'Is the suffering of hell really eternal and conscious?' The purpose of this book isn't to explore the biblical doctrine of hell in detail. For that particular question, I would recommend *Erasing Hell: What God Said about Eternity and the Things We've Made Up* by Francis Chan and Preston Sprinkle (David C. Cook, 2001) – a thorough, honest examination of the biblical data.
† Jer. 6:14 – see also Jer. 8:11 and Ezek. 13:10, 16.
‡ C. S. Lewis, *Mere Christianity* (HarperCollins, 2001), 32.

1

The God Who Cares

It had been a long day. I can't even remember why. I was about eight and as I climbed out of the car, I sighed. Apparently, it was so small that I hadn't even noticed it myself. But then I saw my mother looking at me with a gentle, quizzical smile. 'Are you ok?' She sounded concerned. Despite the myriad of pressing concerns in her grown-up world, not to mention the need to carry in the groceries and juggle so many other balls in that moment, she was paying attention to me. She noticed. She cared. That is our Father. From the minuscule annoyances which no one else notices, to the depths of tragedy which no one else understands, He cares. The psalmist paints an image of this patient, attentive God when he writes that 'Because He bends down to listen, I will pray as long as I have breath.'* Our Father is the parent tenderly stooping to listen as an eight-year-old pours out his troubles.

Your Pain is Precious
'You have kept count of my tossings; put my tears in your bottle. Are they not in your book?'† This verse describes the ancient

---

* Ps. 116:2 (NLT).
† Ps. 56:8.

custom of collecting tears from a time of grief and storing them in a small bottle or 'lachrymatory'. The point was to memorialise the tears as precious and sacred. This is what your Father does. Your grief matters to Him. Every agonised, restless shift in your bed in the small hours has been seen by Him. Every droplet of grief which has trickled down your cheeks has been recorded by Him. He cares. In particular, He cares for His people when they are convulsed by the haunting eternal loss of those they love. Where do we see this in Scripture? Here are three examples.

Elijah

In 1 Kings 19, Elijah has had enough. He wants to end it all. This is one of the few times in the Scripture when a believer is driven to a death-wish. 'It is enough; now, O Lord, take away my life, for I am no better than my fathers.'* 'I have failed to restrain my people's hell-bent idolatry, just like the prophets before me,' he is saying. He vents to God, 'the people of Israel have forsaken your covenant, thrown down your altars, and killed your prophets.'† Elijah is staring into the abyss of his nation's spiritual suicide.

God then comforts and gently corrects him, but why is that conversation even able to happen? Why is Elijah not already a corpse as he had desired? The answer is God's compassion. Elijah had earlier lain down in the wilderness, hoping never to wake again. But then, in one of the most beautiful moments in Scripture, an angel wakes him with a tender physical touch and encourages him to have a warm cake and a jar of water. Elijah partakes, then collapses again. But God doesn't let go. His kindness is too patient and too determined. 'And the angel of

---

* 1 Kings 19:4.
† 1 Kings 19:14.

the Lord came again a second time and touched him and said, "Arise and eat ..."*

In the midst of Elijah's suicidal grief at his people's fatal faithlessness, God cared.

Jeremiah

In 587 B.C., the Babylonians sacked Jerusalem. The event was unspeakably awful, a direct expression of God's judgement. In its aftermath, Jeremiah is plunged into turmoil over the loss of the nation. The book of Lamentations is full of his writhing anguish. Yet the centrepiece of Lamentations is the aspect of God's character to which he clings with these words: 'Because of the Lord's great love we are not consumed, for His compassions never fail. They are new every morning; great is your faithfulness.'†

Re-read that verse. We have a God whose love keeps us from the consuming judgement we all deserve. We have a God of compassion. We have a God whose compassion isn't just an abstract concept doing us little practical good; it manifests itself in specific ways. In other words, He is a God of compassions (plural). We have a God whose compassions are frequent and consistent and trustworthy – as much so as the dawning of each new day. We have a God of unfailing faithfulness.

Paul

Towards the end of his explanation of the gospel in Romans, Paul becomes highly emotional:

> I am speaking the truth in Christ—I am not lying; my conscience bears me witness in the Holy Spirit—that I have great sorrow and

---

* 1 Kings 19:5–7.
† Lam. 3:22.

unceasing anguish in my heart. For I could wish that I myself were accursed and cut off from Christ for the sake of my brothers, my kinsmen according to the flesh.*

This is some of the most intense language in all of Scripture. Paul doesn't just feel sorrow; it's 'great' sorrow. He doesn't just feel anguish; it's 'unceasing' anguish. He doesn't just feel these things on a surface level; he feels them 'in his heart'. In other words, according to the Bible's concept of 'heart', his anguish is more profound than merely emotional. In fact, Paul goes so far as to moot the idea of desiring hell for himself in the place of his brothers, if only it would mean their salvation.

Yet, for all of Paul's anguish, he can rejoice throughout the same letter in a God who miraculously turns our suffering for our good (including when we can't see how);† a God who has laid up eternal glory for us which will eclipse forever even our greatest agonies;‡ a God who is passionately, unstoppably *for* us;§ a God who desires our joy,¶ gives us encouragement,** and who strengthens us.††

With the Philippians, Paul is literally in tears over those whose end is destruction.‡‡ Yet he can then promptly cling to a God who gives joy,§§ who wants to hear our anxious requests,¶¶

---

* Rom. 9:1–3.
† Rom. 5:3–5.
‡ Rom. 8:18.
§ Rom. 8:31.
¶ Rom. 14:17.
** Rom. 15:5.
†† Rom. 16:25.
‡‡ Phil. 3:18.
§§ Phil. 4:4.
¶¶ Phil. 4:6.

a God of peace* and sustaining strength† and loving provision.‡

Consider God's compassion to Elijah and Jeremiah and Paul in the depths of their heartache. Let it sink in – because that same compassion is directed towards you. This is why God preserved the record of His tenderness with them: so that thousands of years later and thousands of miles away, you might read about it here and now, and receive it for yourself. Someone recently wrote to me that Paul's anguish in the verses quoted above 'gave voice to my pain over my Dad's [lack of] salvation long before my Dad ever died. I'm so thankful for these Scriptures!' Lean on these examples of older brothers in the faith who testify to you that amidst the most bitter grief, God cares.

Holy Heartbreak

I knew an elderly woman who came to realise that the gospel was true yet couldn't bring herself to commit to it. This was because she found the destiny of her deceased unbelieving parents hard to acknowledge. She eventually started following Christ, although that meant also taking on this grief.

In the same way, Elijah and Jeremiah and Paul experienced their grief because of their faithfulness. It was an excruciating indicator of their own commitment to the truth of God's judgement. If they had allowed their hearts to harden and for unbelief and apathy to follow, they would have spared themselves this sadness. They would no longer have believed in or cared about the eternal fate of unrepentant rebels. Don't miss this as you consider your own grief. Your pain is a badge of honour. Your sorrow is a testament to your faithfulness. Your heartbreak is holy.

---

* Phil. 4:7.

† Phil. 4:13.

‡ Phil. 4:19.

And your grief is a cost for which you will be reimbursed by Christ many times over. 'Whoever loves his life loses it,' Jesus teaches, 'and whoever hates his life in this world will keep it for eternal life." Hating your life includes opting into the emotional anguish of acknowledging the fate of an unbelieving loved one. Jesus elsewhere promises a 'hundredfold' consolations as well as eternal life.† Those consolations in this life are many and varied and hard to quantify. But they are real. We'll consider some of them later in this book. And although hard to imagine in this world, there will be complete healing in the next.

'It matters to Him about you'

George Muller built orphanages throughout England in the 1800s. By the time of his death, they had served over ten thousand children. His ministry constantly bumped up against seemingly impossible problems. Yet his faith, famous for its passion and power, never wavered. He saw the Lord provide time and again. What sustained this extraordinary faith? Throughout the years, he kept a little motto propped up on his desk: 'It matters to Him about you.'‡ Know that your heavenly Father sees your angst. He cares. It matters to Him about you.

---

* John 12:25.
† Matt. 19:29.
‡ 1 Pet. 5:7.

2

The God Who Grieves

C. S. Lewis knew about grief. He lost friends in the trenches of World War I. He lost his wife to cancer four years into an immensely happy marriage. And as a nine-year-old, he lost the mother who had been his everything. In one heartbreaking passage, he describes a night when he was crying with headache and toothache, distressed because she wasn't coming to him. He was vaguely aware of 'doctors in her room, and voices, and comings and goings all over the house and doors shutting and opening,' none of which he understood. After a several hours, his father came into his room, in tears, 'to try to convey to my terrified mind things it had never conceived before.'* After his mother's death, his relationship with his father broke down, never to recover. Soon afterwards, he was sent away to a brutal boarding school with an abusive headmaster who was later declared insane.

The loss of his mother is echoed in his novel *The Magician's Nephew*: the boy, Digory, has a dying mother back in England and hopes to bring fruit from the land of Narnia to heal her. The lion, Aslan, is the central Christ figure of the book.

* C. S. Lewis, *Surprised by Joy: The Shape of My Early Life* (HarperCollins, 2017), 20.

[Digory] thought of his Mother, and he thought of the great hopes he had had, and how they were all dying away, and a lump came in his throat and tears in his eyes, and he blurted out: 'But please, please – won't you – can't you give me something that will cure Mother?' Up till then he had been looking at the Lion's great front feet and the huge claws on them; now, in his despair, he looked up at its face. What he saw surprised him as much as anything in his whole life. For the tawny face was bent down near his own and (wonder of wonders) great shining tears stood in the Lion's eyes. They were such big, bright tears compared with Digory's own that for a moment he felt as if the Lion must really be sorrier about his Mother than he was himself. 'My son, my son,' said Aslan. 'I know. Grief is great. Only you and I in this land know that yet. Let us be good to one another.'*

Your loss matters to God. But more than simply caring about your grief, He Himself grieves. It is His tragedy too.

God in Flesh

Job questions this. Maybe that's you right now. As Job writhes in anguish which included the loss of children whose spiritual status he was anxious about at best,† he rails against God, bitterly asking 'Have you eyes of flesh? Do you see as man sees?'‡ The stunning answer of the incarnation is 'Yes, yes, yes!'

Picture Christ, fully God and fully man, who, with eyes of flesh, *can* see as man sees. Picture Him breaking down outside the tomb of His friend Lazarus. Spurgeon recalls Tacitus' observation that amber rings were deemed to be without value in ancient Rome – until the Emperor started wearing one, at which point they became prized. Spurgeon continues, 'Bereavements might be looked on as very sad things, but when we recollect that Jesus wept over His friend Lazarus, they are

---

* C. S. Lewis, *The Magician's Nephew* (HarperCollins, 2008), 168.
† Job 1:5.
‡ Job 10:4.

choice jewels ... Christ wore this ring. Then I must not blush to wear it."*

But Christ didn't know only the grief of losing believers He would see again one day, like Lazarus. Luke records Him weeping over the wilfully blind people of Jerusalem, as He foretold their destruction. His prophecy was tragically fulfilled in A.D. 70 when the Romans sacked the city with terrible bloodshed. Christ had been clear about the reason: 'You [Jerusalem] did not know the time of your visitation.'† The city had rejected Him. And this isn't simply Jesus grieving the eternal loss of rebels according to His human nature. This is the Second Person of the Trinity using His divine omniscience to look forty years ahead in history. When we grieve for the lost, we have a God who grieves with us.

Even Apart from the Incarnation
Although the incarnation is a reassuring demonstration of God's compassion, His compassion doesn't hang on it. Listen to His words to Ezekiel, centuries before Christ: 'As I live, declares the Lord God, I have no pleasure in the death of the wicked, but that the wicked turn from his way and live; turn back, turn back [hear the pathos in the repetition] from your evil ways, for why will you die, O house of Israel?'‡

In his book *Grieving: Your Path Back to Peace*, James White describes his friend Mike losing a twenty-nine-day-old granddaughter.§ White describes the funeral, grim beyond words; how wrong it felt to see a tiny baby in a funeral chapel,

---

* Charles Spurgeon, *The Barley-Field on Fire*, Sermon 563, preached 3 April, 1864.
† Luke 19:44.
‡ Ezek. 33:11.
§ I believe we can have confidence in the saving mercy of God for infants – see Chapter 4.

how the cradle was so quickly whisked away in a hearse, how words failed them all. Then White says of his friend, 'Since he opened his heart and loved his granddaughter, Autumn Dawn, he will grieve the loss of that special little girl. Anyone who is old enough to love is old enough to grieve. Fight as we might against it, that is the way God made us.'* That is the way God Himself is too. God made us in His own image. He too grieves because He loves.

The prophet Hosea gives a moving example of this love-fuelled sorrow over a spiritually suicidal people. The book is filled with descriptions of Israel's wickedness and God's judgement. Yet He is agonised by His love for His people: 'It was I who taught Ephraim to walk; I took them up by their arms, but they did not know that I healed them ... How can I give you up, O Ephraim? How can I hand you over, O Israel? ... My heart recoils within me; my compassion grows warm and tender.'†

According to Paul, God 'desires all people to be saved.'‡ According to Peter, God doesn't wish 'that any should perish, but that all should reach repentance.'§ According to Luke, God's desire to rescue extended even to those who put His own Son on the cross.¶ Consider as well the corollary of His ecstatic joy over each sinner who repents;** heart-rending grief over each one who doesn't.

Even Greater Grief

As we've seen, God grieves because God loves. And the height of love correlates to the depth of grief. If I read in the news about

---

* James R. White, *Grieving: Your Path Back to Peace* (Bethany House, 1997), 15.

† Hosea 11:3, 8.

‡ 1 Tim. 2:4.

§ 2 Pet. 3:9.

¶ Luke 7:30.

** Luke 15:10.

an individual dying elsewhere in the country or the world, I'm not particularly moved. If my own son dies, I'm undone. This means, if I may say it gently, that, however great your grief over a lost person might be, God's grief is even greater. For He loved them even more.

He loved them as the One whose capacity for love is infinite, unlike ours. He loved them as the One whose love is perfectly pure and sinless, unlike ours. He loved them as the One who had personally created them. He loved them as the One who had placed His own image upon them. He loved them as the One who had tenderly sustained their brain and lungs and heart moment by moment for a lifetime. He loved them as the One who knew them even better than you did.

If God *Does* Grieve, Why Does He Proceed with Hell?

At this point, you may have a disconcerting question. We've heard much about God's apparent grief over the lost. If it is real, why does He still proceed with casting people into hell? Isn't this contradictory, like an alcoholic weeping over his drunkenness before taking another swig? The answer has two parts: God proceeds with judgement, first, because He is committed to more than one object of love simultaneously (not just His love for rebels); and, second, because He is operating more than one level of will simultaneously (not simply His will for rebels to be saved). This doesn't call into question or cheapen His love for the lost or His desire to show mercy. It does the opposite. It heightens these things, because it shows that they come from a God who is far deeper and grander than we might otherwise think. Let me explain.

More than One Object of Love

As well as loving sinful rebels, God also loves what is good. He loves justice. He loves righteousness. He loves the destruction of evil. He loves the victims of child abuse and rape and torture and murder. The question isn't 'How can a God of love punish some of His creatures?' The question is 'How can He *not*?' He doesn't judge despite His love. He judges *because* of His love. And all of these loves – goodness and justice and righteousness and the destruction of evil and so on – are what He is like by nature. Scripture presents God's glory as the display of His nature, the outworking of His character. So to put this another way, He loves His own glory.

What is more, Scripture presents Him, to use a technical term, as a 'simple' God.[*] That is, His attributes aren't bolt-on parts which are separable from His essential nature. He doesn't merely *have* love or justice or holiness. He *is* love and justice and holiness. His love and justice and holiness are as sure as His existence. His simplicity means that His attributes are inseparable from Him.

It also means that His attributes are inseparable from each other. This prevents us from playing them off against each other. We don't get to choose between His love and His justice and His holiness. His love is a just and holy love; His justice is a loving and holy justice; His holiness is a loving and just holiness – and so on for all of His attributes. We can never rank His attributes in order or say that while He 'is' love, He merely 'has' a blazing, sin-intolerant holiness. The statement 'God *is* love'[†] is no more true than the statement 'God *is* a consuming fire.'[‡]

---

[*] 'God is "simple," that is, sublimely free from all composition, and ... therefore one cannot make any real distinction between his being and his attributes. Each attribute is identical with God's being: he is what he possesses ... Whatever God is, he is that completely and simultaneously.' Herman Bavinck, *Reformed Dogmatics: God and Creation,* trans. John Bolt and John Vriend, vol. 2 (Baker Academic, 2004), 118. For a good introduction to God's nature and the concept of His simplicity, see Matthew Barrett's *None Greater: The Undomesticated Attributes of God* (Baker Books, 2019).

[†] 1 John 4:8.

[‡] Heb. 12:29.

My grandma was a gifted watercolourist. I'll always remember painting sessions as a child when we would sit looking out across her garden. In one vague memory, I can still see her showing me the different primary colours – red, yellow and blue – and how secondary colours derive from those. Loosely, if you don't push the analogy too hard, that's a picture of God's attributes: some are primary while others are secondary derivations of those. For example, in eternity, within the Trinity, God has always had love. He has not always had grief or wrath. Yet these derive from love. His grief is a manifestation of His love (for sinners). His wrath is a manifestation of His love (for the victims of sinners). His grief and wrath are as intrinsic to Him as His love, for they are expressions of His love. They can no less be ranked or played off against each other than His primary attributes.

The Bible forefronts different qualities of God in different situations because this is how His unified, 'simple' character meets us in those various circumstances. Yet He is still all of His qualities maximally and constantly. None of them have to be compromised or contradicted or shut off in order for others of them to be expressed. 'He cannot deny Himself.'* His character knows 'no shadow or variation due to change.'†

Someone might ask, 'But if all of God's character is maximally true all of the time, how come different humans are treated by God differently – some saved and some not?' One of Scripture's answers is that this enables different aspects of God's character to be displayed.‡ Whether a particular aspect of His character rises to the level of effective choice in a given situation doesn't affect whether it is still true and real. He really *does* delight in

---

* 2 Tim. 2:13.

† James 1:17.

‡ Rom. 9:21–23.

mercy* even on the occasions when He chooses to exhibit the fact that He also delights in justice.†

Here's the point: His genuine love for rebels and grief over their destruction does not make His destruction of those rebels contradictory or dysfunctional. His grief is not mutually-exclusive with His judgement. His grief is real.

More than One Level of Will

Not only does God have multiple objects of love simultaneously. He also operates more than one level of will simultaneously. In particular, Scripture distinguishes between two types of will: His sovereign will, sometimes known as His secret will, and His moral will, sometimes known as His revealed will.‡

God's sovereign will is seen in every event that He sovereignly ordains to happen – which is *every* event, right down to the result of a roll of dice.§ He often keeps these events secret from us until they occur. (Think of the dice.) His moral will refers to the things He deems morally right and wrong – the loves and hates which He openly reveals, and commands and forbids in principle. Once one sees this distinction in God's will, it is difficult to unsee, all over Scripture. Here's an obvious example: the Father hates and forbids murder, according to His moral will.⁵ Yet, according to His sovereign will, He ordained it in the form of His Son's death at the hands of the Jews and Romans.**

---

* Micah 7:18.

† Ps. 11:7.

‡ John Piper explores this idea helpfully and in depth in *The Pleasures of God* (Christian Focus, 2001), in the appendix 'Are There Two Wills in God? Divine Election and God's Desire for All to be Saved,' 313–340.

§ Prov. 16:33.

⁵ Exod. 20:13.

** Acts 4:27, 28.

God's desire for the judgement of defiant rebels occurs at the level of His sovereign will. His simultaneous desire that none should perish occurs at the level of His moral will. Both are real. This differentiation may seem strange at first. Yet in fact, it is how we operate ourselves. Picture a good father about to discipline his son. 'This is going to hurt me more than it will hurt you', he might say sadly, before determinedly proceeding. He might even feel satisfaction in the rightness of the act while being sad at the pain caused to his boy. (I remember army medics saying the opposite with classic military humour before carrying out painful procedures: 'This is going to hurt you more than it's going to hurt me!')

Here is the point again: despite the existence of hell, God's grief is real. His multiple objects of love and dual levels of will mean that His judgement of rebels is not self-contradictory. So remember Aslan's tears. We do not grieve alone. We have a God who grieves with us. And despite His judgement, His tears are more significant than any other co-mourner you will ever have.

3

The God Who Knows

In *The Hiding Place*, Corrie Ten Boom describes hiding Jews from the Nazis before she herself endured the horrors of a concentration camp. Early on, she recounts travelling on a train with her father as a young girl and asking him what 'sex sin' is. Just then, the train arrives at their station. He lifts his suitcase from the overhead rack, puts it on the floor, and asks Corrie to carry it off the train for him. She tries to lift it.

> 'It's too heavy,' I said. 'Yes,' he said. 'And it would be a pretty poor father who would ask his little girl to carry such a load. It's the same way, Corrie, with knowledge. Some knowledge is too heavy for children. When you are older and stronger you can bear it. For now you must trust me to carry it for you.' And I was satisfied. More than satisfied – wonderfully at peace. There were answers to this and all my hard questions – for now I was content to leave them in my father's keeping.*

Your Father may have withheld clarity from you about the eternal destiny of someone you cared about. If so, remember that He is a good Father. He doesn't require His children to bear loads too heavy for them. For now you can leave the question

---

* Corrie Ten Boom, *The Hiding Place* (Chosen, 1971), 42.

in His keeping, and this will bring you relief. 'The secret things belong to the Lord our God, but the things that are revealed belong to us.'*

His Purposes in Our Ignorance

By keeping you in ignorance, God could be sparing you from an intolerable emotional burden. In her novel *Middlemarch*, George Eliot writes, '... our frames could hardly bear much of [tragedy]. If we had a keen vision and feeling of all ordinary human life, it would be like hearing the grass grow and the squirrel's heart beat, and we should die of that roar which lies on the other side of silence.'† We would be crushed if God didn't mercifully grant us vast oceans of ignorance in this life.

An interesting illustration of this is the increasingly crushing weight of knowledge we take on through modern technology, social media and the 24-hour news cycle. Our feeble frames are not designed for the omniscience which belongs to God alone, as seen in the rise in recent years of anxiety, depression, preoccupation and other mental health issues. If you've seen the movie *Indiana Jones and the Kingdom of the Crystal Skull* (2008), picture the KGB agent played by Cate Blanchett gaining all the knowledge in the world as she clutches the skull, before her head explodes.

However, if God is keeping you in ignorance, this doesn't necessarily mean that your loved one's fate *was* tragic. Our wise Father will have His reasons for withholding from us the knowledge of another's salvation. He may use our uncertainty over it to spur us to work out our own salvation with fear and trembling, or to equip us to minister to others, or to increase our dependence on him, or to humble and refine us, or to help us in any number of other ways.

---

* Deut. 29:29.

† George Eliot, *Middlemarch* (William Blackwood and Sons, 1871), 109.

So if God has chosen to give us ignorance over another's damnation or salvation, we must try, hard as it may be, to rest in this ignorance. Jesus taught 'Do not be anxious about tomorrow ... Sufficient is the day for its own trouble.'* When God keeps us from knowing a loved one's fate, we can take Jesus' words to include the eternal tomorrow.

And if your Father *has* given you clarity regarding the loss of a blatant unbeliever, you can trust that He will enable you to bear the weight of that load. When Paul was pleading for relief amidst circumstances he could hardly face, God promised him, 'My grace is sufficient for you.'† He says the same to you.

God Alone is Able to Know

Undeniably, fruit gives an indication of someone's true identity and therefore eternal destiny. Jesus teaches that 'a healthy tree cannot bear bad fruit, nor can a diseased tree bear good fruit. Every tree that does not bear good fruit is cut down and thrown into the fire. Thus you will recognize them by their fruits.'‡ Yet He teaches this to enable His listeners to spot false teachers – not to enable them to discern the deepest spiritual realities of everyone around them. Special needs, physical or mental health issues, and other tough personal circumstances can all obscure fruit from our earthly view. A friend of mine believes his mother is saved, but her bipolar disorder makes it difficult for him to see much fruit in her life. And so, while not ignoring the indication of fruit, we must also leave space for the truth that 'the Lord sees not as man sees: man looks on the outward appearance, but the Lord looks on the heart.'§

---

* Matt. 6:34.

† 2 Cor. 12:9.

‡ Matt. 7:18.

§ 1 Sam. 16:7.

Who knows what minuscule seed of saving faith may lurk deep inside a person? Who knows what embryonic trust in Christ may be buried under layers of discouraging appearances to our external observation? Fruit is an indicator of salvation, not an instrument of salvation. Ultimately, salvation is a matter of repentance and faith. That is, it is a matter of the heart. And in the psalmist's words, God alone 'knows the secrets of the heart.'*

God Alone Has the Right to Know

As well as uniquely having the ability to know, God alone has the right to know. Why do I think I have a right to know *anything*? However much I loved someone, why would that obligate God to divulge to me His will for them? If I'm unsure of their fate, a sense of entitlement to know it will only increase my frustration. At the end of John's Gospel, Peter gets impertinent about the future God has planned for John. Peter's demand for that knowledge doesn't go down well with Jesus, who replies, 'What is that to you? You follow me!'† We are called to run our own races, not speculate about the races of others.

Paul was conscious that the standing of others is for the Lord to judge, not us. He challenges the Romans, 'Who are you to pass judgement on the servant of another? It is before his own master [the Lord] that he stands or falls.'‡ He warns the Corinthians, 'Do not pronounce judgment before the time, before the Lord comes, who will bring to light the things now hidden in darkness and will disclose the purposes of the heart.'§ And Paul wasn't above applying this truth to himself: 'What have I to do with judging outsiders? Is it not those inside

---

* Ps. 44:21.

† John 21:22.

‡ Rom. 14:4.

§ 1 Cor. 4:5.

the church who you are to judge [in the sense of discernment regarding church discipline]? *God* judges those outside."* We need to let the judge be the judge.

Deceiving Appearances and Narrow Escapes

And so, even if we fear the worst for someone, we should refrain from being dogmatic. Not for nothing does Scripture talk about people 'escaping through the flames,'† and being 'snatched out of the fire.'‡ Not for nothing does God's Word give us a category for people who, though they are brothers and sisters, need to be addressed as people who 'are still of the flesh.'§ Appearances can be deceiving.

And so there will be surprises in heaven. There will be surprises of exclusion. Think of those who are so committed and spiritual as to prophesy, cast out demons, and 'do many mighty works.' One day, some of them will hear Christ's chilling words, 'I never knew you.'¶ More to our point here, there will also be surprises of inclusion. I recently read about the conversion of a sixty-four-year-old man in Edinburgh whose parents had died years earlier, heartbroken over their son's rejection of their faith. Or think of the Pharisee – a nailed-on certainty for heaven in the eyes of many in his society – who thanked God that he wasn't like 'this tax collector,' before going home unjustified while the latter went home justified.** As Jesus observed, 'The tax collectors and the prostitutes go into the

---

* 1 Cor. 5:12, 13.
† 1 Cor. 3:15.
‡ Jude 23.
§ 1 Cor. 3:1, 3.
¶ Matt. 7:22, 23.
** Luke 18:11.

kingdom of God before you [chief priests and elders]!'* John Newton said it well: 'If I ever reach heaven, I expect to find three wonders there: first, to meet some I had not thought to see there, second to miss some I had expected to see there, and third, the greatest Wonder of all, to find myself there.'†

And heaven's surprises won't only include deceiving appearances. They'll also include narrow escapes. Imagine that you're in the crowd watching the crucifixion. You know that the men either side of Jesus have been found guilty and sentenced as dangerous criminals. Both men are dying as they speak. You're not close enough to hear the croaked words of the first. All you can make out is the more audible railing of the second, defiant and bitter towards Jesus to the last.‡ To all appearances, both men are in the same category. Years later, to your astonishment, you encounter one of them in heaven. (Indeed, what's not to say that, unrecorded by Scripture, the second thief also later repented in his final moments, and that he surprises us all in the next world?)

Consider eighteenth-century New England farmer Luke Short. He gave his life to Christ aged one hundred and three while sitting in a field on his own, reflecting on a sermon he had heard as a teenager, eighty-five years earlier. An ex-film actor whom I met through my church's door-to-door evangelism was soundly converted to Christ in his seventies, just weeks before dementia started to overtake him. He became a committed member of our congregation, and seeing the humble joy which filled the final season of his life never failed to move me.

---

* Matt. 21:31.

† *The Amazing Works of John Newton: Words of Grace and Encouragement from the Famous Hymn Writer,* (Bridge-Logos, 2009), 338.

‡ Luke 23:39–43.

'Escaping through the flames.' We do well not to assume what may have happened in people's minds and hearts in their final moments: 'Betwixt the stirrup and the ground, mercy I ask'd; mercy I found.'*

We should never suggest or encourage a future deathbed conversion to someone who is rejecting Christ. That is a horrifyingly dangerous game to play. The unbeliever who plans to wait for the last moment to repent will likely find that their heart has been hardened and they can't.[†] Likewise, we should never affirm someone who professes Christ but whose lifestyle suggests otherwise. Carnal living despite apparent faith is a similarly horrifying game to play.[‡] Planning for a deceiving appearance is as foolish as planning for a narrow escape. And yet, and yet – none of this can discount the possibility of either. We have a God of astounding grace.

In Summary

The visible fruit of someone's life is an important indicator without which we couldn't function as healthy believers. It enables us to know how to assess and how to disciple this person, whether to warn that person, how to pray for this other person, whether to avoid that teacher who may be false, and so on. Rarely is smoke without fire. Yet, in the final analysis, we can only see outward appearances. It is the Lord who looks on the heart.

---

* From *Epitaph for a Man Killed by Falling* by William Camden (1551–1623).

† God has a way of handing rebels over to their own rebellion. Rom. 1:24,26,28. For example, and to pull on a fascinating thread, trace the hardening of Pharoah's heart, fundamentally by God in judgement, but within that, by Pharoah himself: Exodus 4:21; 7:3; 7:13; 7:14; 7:22; 8:15; 8:19; 8:32; 9:7; 9:12; 9:34; 9:35; 10:1; 10:20; 10:27; 11:10; 14:4; 14:5, 14:8.

‡ James 2:14.

When He seems to make someone's doom agonisingly apparent, we can trust Him to sustain us under that emotional burden. When He instead decides to leave us with uncertainty, we can trust that His purposes towards us are deliberate and perfect. He is a good Father who will neither place a weight of knowledge upon us that we cannot bear (in the case of someone's eternal loss) – nor a weight of knowledge which for some reason may not be for our best (in the case of someone's surprising salvation). Like Corrie Ten Boom, we can rest in the truth that these things are for our Father to know, and for Him to reveal to us or not, in His wise providence.

4

The God Who Judges

Let the Judge be the Judge

It is not the place of this book to examine in detail the doctrine of hell. For that, I would recommend the books footnoted here.* But one key principle is that God's judgement will be fair. 'Shall not the Judge of all the earth do what is just?'† We shouldn't expect always to understand what justice looks like. We would be God if we did. The more we can humbly allow God to be God, and to rest in that, even when we can't fathom His actions, the more we will experience relief. God knows what He is doing, and we must let the judge be the judge.

We must also be careful not to assume undue responsibility upon ourselves when others go to hell. In the end, rebels have themselves to blame. In Ezekiel's words, 'the wickedness of the

---

* Edward Donnelly, *Biblical Teaching on the Doctrines of Heaven and Hell* (Banner of Truth, 2001); John Blanchard, *Whatever Happened to Hell?* (Evangelical Press, 1993); Francis Chan and Preston Sprinkle, *Erasing Hell: What God Said about Eternity and the Things We've Made Up* (David C. Cook, 2011); Dane Ortlund, *Is Hell Real?* (9 Marks, 2022); Erik Raymond, *Is Hell For Real?* (The Good Book Company, 2017).

† Gen. 18:25.

wicked shall be upon himself.'* There is a degree of responsibility we bear when we shirk opportunities to witness – as Ezekiel also acknowledges† – but final responsibility rests with the people who themselves willfully rejects God. Edward Donnelly is helpful here: 'Do not accept more responsibility than that which God puts on you. If you do, it will break you ... We need not be afraid that, if we do not immediately evangelize everyone we know, they will drop into hell by mistake. Christ will save every one of His chosen people.'‡ Of course, we sometimes fail as witnesses to our children, our parents, our friends. We cannot agonise and fixate on that unhealthily. If we have failed to witness faithfully, we must receive God's grace and forgiveness, acknowledge His absolute sovereignty over salvation, accept that rebels bear final responsibility for themselves, and once again, let the judge be the judge.

What about Predestination?

I wonder what you make of the paradox in the last sentence, the claim *both* that God has 'absolute sovereignty over salvation' *and* that 'rebels bear final responsibility for themselves'?

Predestination is the truth celebrated throughout Scripture that God safely secured His people even before time began. 'In love, He predestined us for adoption to Himself ...';§ 'In Him we have obtained an inheritance, having been predestined ...';¶ 'Those whom He foreknew He also predestined ... and those whom He predestined He also called ...'** Many of the Old

* Ezek. 18:20.
† Ezek. 33:8, 9.
‡ Edward Donnelly, *Biblical Teaching on the Doctrines of Heaven and Hell* (Banner of Truth, 2001), 60.
§ Eph. 1:4, 5.
¶ Eph. 1:11.
** Rom. 8:29, 30.

Testament and all of the New Testament writers reference this truth.* But it raises a troubling corollary: if God actively chose to save some before the world began, doesn't that mean, effectively, that He chose for others to reject Him? And if so, how can they then be blamed for rejecting Him? How is that fair?

The Bible is clear that our choices are real.† They are real in the sense that we choose what we genuinely desire to choose.‡ This is not the same as saying that our choices are free, because God's sovereignty extends to all things, including our desires.§ The idea of being absolutely free from a God of absolute sovereignty is incoherent. Our freedom and God's sovereignty are mutually exclusive, by definition. 'In Him we live and move and have our being.'¶ To want freedom from Him is like a fish wanting freedom from water. God is sovereign *and* our choices are real.

This means that rebels, notwithstanding God's sovereignty, are never guiltless.** There is admittedly a paradox here. So, if we deem this reality to be morally or intellectually nonsensical, we need to decide whether we think that God (wise and good infinitely beyond our understanding) is mistaken and we are right – or whether we (with limited, fallen hearts and minds) are mistaken and He is right. The fact that a three-year-old doesn't like or comprehend the realities of brain surgery doesn't make brain surgery foolish or wrong. We are the three-year-old and He is the brain surgeon. If the truthfulness or rightness

---

* Examples, far from exhaustive, from each New Testament writer (other than Paul, already cited) include Matt. 24:22; Mark 13:27; Luke 18:7; John 15:6,7; Heb. 2:13; James 2:5; 1 Pet. 1:1; Jude 4.

† Acts 2:37–40.

‡ Josh. 24:15.

§ Phil. 2:13.

¶ Acts 17:28.

** Rom. 1:20.

of something *did* depend on our complete understanding and approval of it, God would be very small. He would also be a god we had made in our own image.

Jesus Himself, especially throughout John's gospel, is particularly clear on both the sovereignty of God and the simultaneous culpability of those who reject Him. One example: 'Everyone who does wicked things hates the light and does not come to the light, lest his works should be exposed.' In other words, rebels are culpable. Jesus promptly continues, 'But whoever does what is true comes to the light, so that it may be clearly seen that his works have been *carried out in God*' – that is, carried out by God's will and power.

It is never as if those whom God didn't choose for salvation later find themselves desperately repenting and believing but being turned away. Jesus promises that 'whoever comes to me I will never cast out.'[†] But His words immediately beforehand reiterate that anyone only ever comes to Him because of God's sovereignty: 'All that the Father gives me will come to me.'[‡]

So, to answer the questions at the start of this section: yes, God chose for some not to be saved.[§] And no, God's choice for some not to be saved wasn't unfair. Fairness, by definition, is what God does. He isn't judged by it. He decides it. Right is right *because* God does it. God is fair like water is wet. It is who He is. In any case, people who were not predestined for

---

[*] John 3:20, 21.

[†] John 6:37b.

[‡] John 6:37a.

[§] Prov. 16:4; John 17:12; Rom. 9:17,18; 1 Pet. 2:8. It is important to note, however, that God's choice for some to be lost isn't parallel or symmetrical for His choice for some to be saved. This is a deeper discussion, helpfully summarised by R. C. Sproul in his article 'Is Double Presdestination Biblical?', Ligonier, www.ligonier.org/learn/articles/double-predestination-biblical. Accessed 3 August, 2023.

salvation are not missing out on anything to which they had a right. The very nature of God's saving grace and mercy is that they are undeserved. And in rejecting God, rebels are pursuing what they truly want.

How is it that divine sovereignty doesn't negate human responsibility or override human culpability? More could be said about this paradox. But in the end, we have to be humble before the God whose wisdom and goodness far exceed our scope to understand.* We have to acknowledge reality in the way that He has set it up. At the end of his discussion of these very things in Romans 9–11, Paul admits, 'Oh, the depth of the riches and wisdom and knowledge of God! How unsearchable are His judgments and how inscrutable His ways! "For who has known the mind of the Lord, or who has been His counsellor?"'† The only thing left is to recognise, humbly, God's utter sovereignty over all things, and to worship Him accordingly. And this is precisely how Paul concludes: 'For from Him and through Him and to Him are all things. To Him be glory forever. Amen.'‡

As well as difficult theology around God's judgement, we are also confronted with difficult practical scenarios. For example, what about those who commit suicide? What about those who die very young or those who are mentally disabled? Let's consider these questions in turn now.

Suicide

Last night, while driving home from work, I had a surreal experience. I spotted a man about to jump off a bridge over a busy motorway, and thankfully managed to stop him. He refused to tell me his name or anything about himself, and I

---

* Job 26:14.

† Rom. 11:33, 34.

‡ Rom. 11:36.

had to leave when the police arrived. All I can remember about him is that he was wearing socks but no shoes. All night I thought about others I've known over the years who have killed themselves, some of them believers. Then I woke this morning to a text from someone in my church small group asking for prayer because his son's teammate had taken his own life. What are we to make of God's judgement in relation to suicide?

The idea that suicide is the unforgiveable sin is cruel and wrong. According to Scripture, the only sin which cannot receive God's forgiveness is ... refusing God's forgiveness! In other words, the unforgiveable sin is definitively rejecting the Holy Spirit, by whom we would have been able to repent and receive that forgiveness.* Christians, by definition, aren't guilty of the unforgiveable sin. Non-Christians, by definition, are.

Some believe that suicide is unforgiveable because it doesn't leave any chance for repentance afterwards. This is dangerously mistaken logic. When Christ died, His death paid for all of His people's sins, past, present *and future*. As a believer, my salvation was secured from before the foundation of the world.† Through justification by faith, my status changed at my initial conversion from sinful to righteous, fully and forever.‡ At the point of death, Christ didn't shout in victory, 'It is finished ... as long as you remember to keep repenting after each sin so that we don't miss any.' We *all* die with probably millions of specific sins for which we haven't repented. In any case, it isn't our repeated repentance but Christ's constant intercession which continually applies His death to our sin.§ No, He roared in triumph, simply, 'It is finished!'⁑ For the believer, 'neither death

---

* Mark 3:28–30, Matt. 12:32.

† Eph. 1:4, 5.

‡ Rom. 5:9.

§ Heb. 7:25.

⁑ John 19:30.

nor life ... nor things present nor things to come [including future sins for example] ... nor anything else in all creation will be able to separate us from the love of God in Christ."*

Suicide is undeniably a sin, assuming the individual had enough mental capacity to be at least partially responsible for their act of self-murder. Yet, interestingly, in all six of the Bible's recorded suicides, none has explicit moral evaluation attached.[†] I take from this that, when people have been driven to the point of taking their life, their mental and emotional state means we should be cautious in our own judgement of their final act. Only the Lord knows the exact diminishment of their responsibility because of the pain or delusion they were suffering. We can trust that His flawless fairness will extend to victims of suicide, whether they were saved or not.

Infants and Others without Mental Capacity

Writer Kent Aldershof describes visiting friends in the Philippines, the parents of a little girl with anencephaly. She had no brain except for the sub-brain attached to the spinal cord enabling involuntary actions such as breathing. When Kent arrived, his friends led him into their daughter's room to see her.

> The girl was lying on a bed, in a beautifully furnished bedroom. She was dressed in a lovely dark blue velvet dress, with a white lace collar. Her hair was full and fluffy, undoubtedly to disguise that the top of her skull was unformed or in a manner of speaking, collapsed. She did not move nor react. She did nothing but lie there and breathe, which in fact was all she could do. To answer

---

* Rom. 8:38, 39.

† Abimelech in Judg. 9:50–57; Samson in Judg. 16:28–30 (whether this is strictly suicide is debatable); Saul and his armour-bearer in 1 Sam. 31:1–6 (2 Sam. 1:1–15; 1 Chronicles 10:1–13); Ahithophel in 2 Sam. 17:23; Zimri in 1 Kings 16:18, 19; Judas Iscariot in Matt. 27:5.

your question, she was beautiful. One of the prettiest little girls I have ever seen. Gorgeous little cupid-bow lips, long dark eyelashes, smooth and bright skin, and a perfectly formed body. An ideal child, whom anyone would love. Except that she had no brain. She was blind, deaf, dumb, and could feel no pain. She could not move.*

How will God judge that little girl? How will He judge the victim of an abortion, the stillborn, the newborn, someone of *any* age who lacked the mental capacity to understand His witness of creation and conscience? We need to tread humbly here because God's Word isn't as clear as in other areas. Yet there is cause for confidence in God's saving grace. And even if there is any haze of ambiguity, we can still trust that God is good and fair and wise beyond our imaginings, and justified in all that He does.

I don't believe that those without mental capacity are saved because they aren't sinful. They are. Humans are '*by nature* children of [God's] wrath' for sin, asserts Paul.† 'I was brought forth in iniquity, and in sin did my mother conceive me' admits David.‡ Yet Scripture does suggest that God extends His saving mercy through Christ to those who didn't reject the witness of creation and conscience by which others are condemned – those who, though sinful in nature, are not sinful in practice.

Listen, for example, to God's reasoning in Deuteronomy 1. His people are rejecting Him and failing to trust Him to give them the land of Canaan. In judgement, God bars them from the Promised Land. Yet He is careful to exclude their 'little ones' from this punishment because, He says, they have 'no

---

* https://www.quora.com/Who-has-the-lowest-IQ-in-the-world Accessed 15 March 2023.

† Eph. 2:3.

‡ Ps. 51:5.

knowledge of good or evil.' He says instead that 'I *will* give [the Promised Land], and they shall possess it.'* Scripture presents the New Creation as our Promised Land,† and it seems right to apply God's reasoning to 'little ones' today, who likewise have 'no knowledge of good or evil.'‡

Paul implies something similar in Romans 1, where he describes how humanity deserves God's wrath for rejecting God's witness.

In his argument, Paul first cites the witness of creation: '[God's] ... attributes, namely, His eternal power and divine nature, have been clearly perceived, ever since the creation of the world, in the things that have been made. So they are without excuse.'§ Presumably then, someone who *hasn't* perceived His attributes because they *haven't* seen the things that have been made is *not* without excuse.

Next, Paul cites the witness of conscience: 'Though they know God's righteous decree that those who practice such things deserve to die, they [do them].'¶ Again, presumably then, someone who *doesn't* know this because they *don't* have the self-awareness of a functioning conscience *doesn't* deserve to die.

Finally, Paul gives examples of sins flowing from a willful rejection of the dual witness of creation and conscience: idolatry,

---

* Deut. 1:39, emphasis added.

† Heb. 3:16–19.

‡ Someone might point out that the only 'little ones' in Deut. 1 are those within God's visible people, the equivalent of the church today. They might therefore object to the implication of salvation for *all* infants, including those outside the church. Yet it is difficult to see why the principle of being too young to have 'knowledge of good or evil' (the stated reason in Deut. 1 for the suspension of judgement) would suddenly stop being true of humans outside of the visible covenant community, then or now.

§ Rom. 1:20.

¶ Rom. 1:32.

envy, deceit, gossip, slander, haughtiness, boastfulness, giving approval to others who sin, and so on.[*] In Paul's argument, it is 'those who do such things [who] deserve to die'.[†] This begs the question about those who because of age or capacity *don't* and in fact *can't* 'do such things'.

Undoubtedly, the blood of Christ is the only way of salvation. 'There is no other name under heaven ... by which we must be saved'.[‡] So, given the direction that Scriptures like Deuteronomy 1 and Romans 1 push us, it seems reasonable to trust that God somehow applies the saving death of Christ to those without the mental capacity to reject Him. But how can He do this if they are unable to express faith, by which salvation is received? Perhaps the mysterious way that John the Baptist could be filled by the Spirit while still in Elizabeth's womb is indicative.[§]

Our cause for optimism is further strengthened when we consider God's character – that He 'delivers ... him who has no helper [and] has pity on the weak and the needy';[¶] that He rejoices over the salvation of the lost;[**] that He is 'merciful and gracious, slow to anger and abounding in steadfast love and faithfulness';[††] that He loves to save people 'to the praise of His glorious grace'.[‡‡]

In particular, Scripture shows us a God with an especially tender heart towards children,[§§] a God who ordains praise

---

[*] Rom. 1:23–32.

[†] Rom. 1:32.

[‡] Acts 4:12.

[§] Luke 1:15.

[¶] Ps. 72:12, 13.

[**] Luke 15:32.

[††] Ps. 86:15.

[‡‡] Eph. 1:6.

[§§] Mark 9:36, 37; 10:13–16.

for Himself 'out of the mouth of infants and nursing babies.'*
It is striking that Jesus would physically call children over to
Himself while teaching and then say things like, 'It is not the
will of my Father who is in heaven that one of these little ones
should perish'† and 'Do not despise one of these little ones. For
I tell you that in heaven their angels always see the face of my
Father who is in heaven.'‡

King David was confident that he would one day be reunited
with his baby boy.§ I believe we can share that confidence
regarding all who similarly lack the capacity to reject God's
witness, from the zygote, to the anencephalic child, to the
person with severe brain damage.

Regarding infants in particular, consider history's extreme
infant mortality rates and the abortion holocaust of the last
half-century. It is striking to think that if those who are guiltless
of rejecting God's witness *are* saved, in the world to come they
will greatly outnumber we whose lives in this world were self-
consciously Christian. Musing on this, Charles Spurgeon said,
'It is a sweet belief to my own mind that there will be more saved
than lost, for in all things Christ is to have the pre-eminence, and
why not in this?'¶ I marvel at the prospect one day of the sight of
many billions of redeemed, perfected foetuses and babies and
those with severe disabilities in this life. Wouldn't that be so like
the Lord? Wouldn't that be so like the One who loves to choose
the foolish (even those with an IQ of 1) to shame the wise, and
the weak to shame the strong, and what is low and despised so
that none may boast?**

* Matt. 21:16; Ps. 8:2.

† Matt. 18:14.

‡ Matt. 18:10.

§ 2 Sam. 12:23.

¶ Charles Spurgeon, *Infant Salvation*, Sermon 411, preached on
29 September, 1861.

** 1 Cor. 1:27–29.

Whatever the case, we can be certain that God will judge all people in a way that is right and fair and good, for He Himself is the standard of rightness and fairness and goodness. 'His work is perfect, for all His ways are justice. A God of faithfulness and without iniquity, just and upright is He.'*

An early draft of this book included two extra chapters exploring in depth the doctrine of hell. They weren't appropriate for the specific pastoral aim of this book, so I'm glad the editor persuaded me to leave them out. But let me be honest: the truths they covered cost me much sleep and caused me much prayer. The prospect of people going to hell brought Christ Himself to tears. Be reassured if you find the idea of judgement difficult. Like God Himself, we too love sinners. This is a healthy, God-honouring thing. If this love is what is causing our difficulty with hell (and not thinking we know better than God, or distrusting Scripture, or idolising an unbeliever), then our difficulty with hell is likewise a healthy, God-honouring thing. As we'll see in the next chapter, there will come a day when we will feel differently about this doctrine. For now, we can be reassured if we find hell hard.

---

* Deut. 32:4.

5

The God Who Heals

Wrestling with God in the night, Jacob had his hip dislocated and was left with a limp for the rest of his life.[*] Perhaps you feel you've gone through something similar: a grapple with God in deep darkness over the doctrine of hell and His judgement of someone you loved. Perhaps you have an emotional limp which you can't imagine shedding. Maybe you never quite will in this life. I wouldn't be so crass as to promise you otherwise. Yet, as Jacob could also attest, those who come to God in faith, determined to experience His goodness and ready to trust His pain, always leave with blessing, one way or another.[†] And in the life to come, there will be no limps.

There are several ways in which God will salve your grief in this life, and we'll explore some of these shortly. But first, we need to know that, as well as real healing in this world, there will be perfect healing in the next. Our good Father really will wipe away *every* tear – there really will be *no* more mourning nor crying nor pain.[‡] In David's words, 'You who have made me

---

[*] Gen. 32:24–32.
[†] Heb. 11:16.
[‡] Rev. 21:4.

see many troubles and calamities will revive me again; from the depths of the earth you will bring me up again.'[*]

Perfect Healing in Eternity

Humans are more like mirrors than torches. We're more like the moon than the sun. Any light of attractiveness or goodness or lovability isn't ultimately generated from us or created in us. It's reflected by us. It comes from the One who is the source of light – the One apart from whom we have no good thing.[†] It was God's grace in unbelievers which made them lovable to us in this life. In judgement, they will be cut off from that grace.[‡] God's light will be withdrawn from them. So the reasons for which we loved them will therefore no longer be true of them. In some sense at least, from our point of view, they will be different people from those we knew in this life. Those who reject Christ in this world will no longer *be* our loved ones.

So we do well to remember, in C. S. Lewis's words, that 'the dullest and most uninteresting person you can talk to may one day be a creature which, if you saw it now, you would be strongly tempted to worship, or else a horror and a corruption such as you now meet, if at all, only in a nightmare.'[§] Believers can echo the sentiment of Victor Hugo's famous words, 'I am the tadpole of an archangel.' We are currently tadpoles loving tadpoles. If I may say it gently, archangels don't miss tadpoles.

What's more, in losing some of the human reflections of God's grace in this world, we will gain the source of that grace Himself in the next. The New Jerusalem 'has no need of sun or moon to shine on it, for the glory of God gives it light.'[¶] God

[*] Ps. 71:20.

[†] Ps. 16:2.

[‡] 2 Thess. 1:9.

[§] C. S. Lewis, *The Weight of Glory* (HarperCollins, 2001), 45.

[¶] Rev. 21:23.

blesses us in this world with reflections of His light – 'sun and moon to shine on it' we might say – deep friendships (including with unbelievers) and music and sport and good food and beautiful weather and great literature and so on. In the next world, we will bask in His beam directly.

There will still be tangible pleasures and human relationships to enjoy in the New Creation – far greater ones than in this creation in fact. But they will be nothing compared to the Fount from whom them come, whom we will have more intimately and directly than ever before. In Lewis' words, 'In Heaven there will be no anguish and no duty of turning away from our earthly Beloveds ... because we shall have turned already; from the portraits to the Original, from the rivulets to the Fountain, from the creatures He made lovable to Love Himself.'* Two hundred years earlier, Jonathan Edwards rejoiced in the same truth:

> To go to heaven, fully to enjoy God, is infinitely better than the most pleasant accommodations here. Better than fathers and mothers, husbands, wives, or children, or the company of ... all earthly friends. These are but shadows; but God is the substance. These are but scattered beams; but God is the sun. These are but streams; but God is the fountain. These are but drops; but God is the ocean.[†]

Perfect Healing will Include 'Hallelujah'

Now we need to allow God's Word to push us further: not only will our happiness be unclouded *regardless* of God's judgement. It will be cloudless *because* of God's judgement.

I once heard about a pastor's account of an elderly woman he knew, speaking on her deathbed to her son. She was broken-

---

* C. S. Lewis, *The Four Loves* (Harcourt, 1960), 139.
† Jonathan Edwards, *The Works of Jonathan Edwards (Volume 17): Sermons and Discourses 1730–1733*; Mark Valeri (ed.), (Yale University Press, 1999), 437,438.

hearted about her son's rejection of the gospel. Her final words were to warn him through tears that, although she loved him and grieved his damnation, she knew she would one day rejoice at God's judgement of him. Not just that she would rejoice within her own unblemished happiness – but rejoice *at God's judgement of him*. How could she say such a thing? Was she being cruel or deranged or manipulative? She was being biblical.

The word 'Hallelujah' literally means 'Praise God!' It appears four times in the New Testament, and the occasion of each is God's final judgement.* These 'Hallelujahs' are uttered by believers, not in this world, but in the next. So this is not an emotional response to a person's damnation for us to emulate now. But one day, hard to imagine from our current perspective, it will be. We will perceive God's actions with perfected hearts and minds. We will finally see the true horror of defiant sin. We will perceive the terrible beauty of God's dazzling glory in its destruction. We will understand and respond to the display of His justice and holiness with new capacity. Our joy and God's judgement will be joined. Not only will our happiness not be fettered by it. It will be fueled by it.

This isn't an argument based on a single word study. The entire book of Revelation, giving us a glimpse into the next world, is saturated with our joy alongside His judgment, our praise alongside His punishment. 'Fear God and give Him glory, because the hour of His judgment has come, and worship Him...'† 'Great and amazing are your deeds O Lord God Almighty!' [in the context of deadly plagues manifesting 'the wrath of God']‡ 'Rejoice over her [the city of rebellion]...you saints and apostles and prophets, for God has given judgement for you against her.'§

---

* Rev. 19:1–6.
† Rev. 14:7.
‡ Rev. 15:3.
§ Rev. 18:20.

And this theme isn't even just specific to Revelation. It's Bible-wide. It's the same idea foreshadowed in Moses' joy over the destruction of the Egyptians,* and David's joy over the judgement of the wicked,† and the righteous shouting for joy when the wicked perish in Proverbs,‡ and Jeremiah's call to rejoice over Babylon's destruction,§ and the Jews' feasting and gladness at the annihilation of those who had tried to wipe them out under Queen Esther.¶ Hard as it may be to feel or imagine now, the eternal display of God's justice and holiness in the eternal destruction of the wicked will result in the eternal praise and joy of His people.

Real Healing in this Life

We've just thought about healing in the form of flawless joy in the world to come. Yet there is comfort available in this one as well. Perfect healing in the future, yet still real healing now. What does this look like?

For one thing, the more we look to our eternal future, the more it will yield comfort and hope and perspective in the present. Maybe we will still limp like Jacob – but there will be solace in the suffering. It was 'for the joy that was set before him' that Christ was able to able to endure in the meantime,** and the writer to the Hebrews urges us to sustain ourselves in the same way. Jonathan Edwards would apparently pray often, 'Lord, stamp my eyeballs with eternity.' That is a good prayer.

For another thing, God extends to us various means of

---

* Exod. 15:1–21.

† Ps. 58:10.

‡ Prov. 11:10.

§ Jer. 51:48.

¶ Esther 9:16–19.

** Heb. 12:2.

grace. Scripture will offer all kinds of deep comfort when we give ourselves to serious study. Prolonged prayer will bring the supernatural 'peace of God which surpasses all understanding.'* Fellowship will make available the love and support of other believers, as well as the relief which comes from taking our eyes off ourselves and ministering to others.

Comfort will also come in this life through the knowledge that He is using our loss to refine us, to bless others, and to glorify Himself. Let's look at these three ideas in turn.

Know that He is Refining You

Kintsugi is the Japanese art of repairing tea bowls using liquid gold or silver. Tea masters use the precious metals to cement the broken pieces back together. This results in rivulets which highlight the scars as part of the new design, producing stronger, more beautiful bowls than before they were broken.

Trust the One who 'heals the brokenhearted and binds up their wounds.'† Trust Him to use your brokenness to make you more beautiful and stronger and wiser and more useful. He did this for Paul. In 2 Corinthians 4, Paul wasn't just *sustained* through his brokenness – 'afflicted in every way, but not crushed; perplexed, but not driven to despair ... struck down, but not destroyed'‡ – he was *enhanced* through his brokenness: it was precisely *by* 'carrying in [his] body the death of Jesus' (his suffering) that he was able to manifest Jesus' life to others.§ It was *by* 'being given over to death for Jesus' sake' (that is, suffering) that he was able to minister life to others.¶

---

* Phil. 4:6, 7.

† Ps. 147:3.

‡ 2 Cor. 4:8, 9.

§ 2 Cor. 4:10.

¶ 2 Cor. 4:11.

A key to redeeming your pain now is to know that God is using it to work on you in vital, beautiful ways. Perhaps, like Paul, He is equipping you to minister to others. Perhaps He is weaning you off the idolatry of another human which would otherwise have been spiritually fatal. Perhaps He is awakening in you a courage and urgency for evangelism which He will use to bring many to eternal life. Perhaps He is giving you a realism about the seriousness of sin, or an appreciation of His glory, or an urgency for your own salvation which will change the rest of your life. Perhaps, as the Apostle Peter describes, He is refining your faith in the fire of your grief, for the sake of more praise and honour when you finally meet Christ.* Perhaps He is doing any number of other things. Whether or not you see them now, rest assured: He is refining you.

Know that He is Blessing Others
One evening in the Summer of 1808, a young man called Adoniram Judson arrived at a country inn while journeying to visit his uncle. He had been raised in a Christian home but, on his twentieth birthday, had broken his parents' hearts by announcing his rejection of their faith. His best friend, Jacob Eames, had led him away from the gospel into deism. When Judson arrived at the inn, the innkeeper warned that he might be kept awake by the ill man in the next-door room. All night, Judson had to listen to the man spluttering and gasping for air. By morning, the noises had gone. As Judson was leaving, he enquired if the man had recovered. He was told that the man had died. Judson asked who he had been. 'A man called Jacob Eames,' the innkeeper replied. Judson was stunned. According to one biographer, 'He stayed there for hours, pondering the death of his unbelieving friend. If Eames were right [about

---

* 1 Pet. 1:7.

deism], then this was a meaningless event. But Judson could not believe it.'* To quote another biographer, 'That hell should open in that country inn, and snatch Jacob Eames, his dearest friend and guide, from the next bed, this could not – simply could not – be coincidence.'†

The event triggered Judson's conversion within three months. He attended seminary and then spent the remaining thirty-eight years of his life as a missionary to the unreached people of Myanmar (then Burma). By the time he died, his fruit included the translation of the entire Bible into Burmese, an English-Burmese dictionary, hundreds of converts to Christ, and the embryonic beginnings of what is today the Myanmar Baptist Convention. In 2020, this denomination numbered over 5,300 churches and over a million members.‡ Scripture insists that God works 'all things' together for good.§ 'All things' includes the tragedy of others going to hell.

In 1969, my wife's great-grandfather, Newton Howell, was killed in a high-speed car crash. Newton's adult son, Don, was inconsolable at the funeral. God hadn't apparently been more than nominal in the family, but the event caused Don to start thinking more seriously about life and death. He began reading the Scriptures in earnest. Soon afterwards, he understood the gospel for the first time and placed his faith in Christ. He placed a large sign at the entrance of his business quoting Romans 5:8: 'But God shows his love for us in that while we were still sinners, Christ died for us.'

---

* John Piper, *Filling Up the Afflictions of Christ: The Cost of Bringing the Gospel to the Nations in the Lives of William Tyndale, Adoniram Judson and John Paton* (IVP, 2009), 91.
† Courtney Anderson, *To the Golden Shore: The Life of Adoniram Judson* (Zondervan, 1956), 45.
‡ *https://baptistworld.org/members. Accessed 27 November, 2023.*
§ Rom. 8:28.

Then Don's mother, Newton's wife, returned to the faith of her childhood and was baptised at the age of seventy. Don's wife Barbara, in turn, was saved. Because of Don's and Barbara's conversions, now their children, Newton's grandchildren, were growing up to know and fear the Lord. One of those grandchildren, my father-in-law, went into church planting and seminary teaching among unreached people. The grandchildren married believers and have raised believers, and those great grandchildren, in turn, have married believers and are raising believers. What is more, a significant proportion of these people are in full-time ministry, helping usher others in turn to heaven.

Throughout all of this, Don's business experienced God's massive blessing and he began systematically giving away vast amounts of money. By the time he entered heaven aged ninety-four in 2021 (preceded ten days earlier by his wife Barbara), he had funded gospel ministries all over the world. He had also set up a ministry within Georgia's education system, through which many young people have come to Christ, and which continues bearing fruit to this day. All from the sobering loss of his father in a car crash half a century earlier.

There's no knowing how God may use the loss of one person for the blessing of others. There's no knowing when or if you will get to see that blessing this side of eternity. But rest assured that God is doing what God does, working all things – even the eternal loss of someone you cared about – for good.

Know that He is Glorifying Himself

For those who fear they have lost loved ones to an unthinkable eternity, healing in this life is also available in the knowledge that in all things, even including this, God is glorifying Himself. This may seem grotesque at first. Yet the glory of God is the single most important idea for understanding and coping with the eternal loss of others. The glory of God is in fact the bottom line of all of Scripture and all of the universe. And it is this idea to which we turn now.

6

The God Who Self-Glorifies

When I was a boy, we had a family friend who had served in
World War II as a platoon commander. At the end of June 1944,
he was involved in the push through France, and was shot by
a German sniper. Astonishingly, he survived, despite the bullet
entering the bridge of his nose at a sharp angle and exiting
below his ear. (As an old man, he would place one of my fingers
on each scar and remark with a wink that luckily there had been
nothing of value between the bullet's entry and exit points.)
After the shooting, a German soldier ran over to inspect him
before leaving him for dead. But he was able to glance up at the
soldier's belt and read the inscription engraved on the buckle,
'Gott Mit Uns' – 'God With Us'. And all he could think at the
time was, 'But I thought God was with *us!*'

Fundamentally, God isn't for particular nations or
denominations or organisations. *Fundamentally*, God isn't even
for His people. Fundamentally, God is for Himself. Of course
He is for His people, but that's because, first and foremost, He
is for Himself!* Years before my friend's experience in World
War II, another military commander learnt the same lesson:
one day, during the invasion of Canaan, Joshua encountered

* Isa. 48:9–11.

a man wielding a sword. Joshua asked 'Are you for us, or for our adversaries?' and the man replied, 'No! ... I am the commander of the army *of the Lord* ...'* And Joshua fell on his face and worshipped.

God is Great

God is fundamentally for Himself because He is, by definition, the most worthy, valuable Being in existence. If He ever valued anyone or anything above Himself, He would be committing idolatry. He is not being hypocritical in telling us to put Him before ourselves, while refusing to put us before Himself. He is being consistent. Just as He commands us to value Him above all, so He Himself does the same. When we treat ourselves as most important (as we often do), we are being vain and proud and egotistic and idolatrous. When He treats Himself as most important (as He always does), He is being appropriate. He is simply reflecting reality. And so the psalmist can pray, 'Not to us, O Lord, not to us, but to your name give glory.'†

The reason God is the highest, most worthy Being in existence is His nature – His boundless omnipotence and omniscience and omnipresence and eternality and love and wisdom and beauty and everything else about Him. The Bible calls the manifestation – the display – of this nature His 'glory'. The purpose of literally all that God does is His glory.‡ This includes His judgement of unrepentant sinners, for that too displays His nature. In fact, it is striking how clearly and

---

* Josh. 5:13, 14.

† Ps. 115:1.

‡ In Calvin's helpful picture, all the world is a 'platform', a 'dazzling theatre', for God's glory. John Calvin, *The Institutes of the Christian Religion*, ed. John T. McNeill, trans. Ford L. Battles, 2 vols (Westminster John Knox, 1960), 1.14.20; 1.5.8; 6.2.1.

consistently Scriptures ties God's judgement to God's glory.* God's Word shows us how God's judgement displays His power,† and His victory over those who oppose Him,‡ and His fury at those who hurt His people,§ and His supremacy,¶ and His holiness,** and His freedom of action,†† and His wrath against evil‡‡ and (by contrast) His mercy,§§ and His majesty,¶¶ and His righteousness,*** and His avengement of innocent victims.†††

Therefore – and here is the point – the extent to which we

---

* A representative snapshot from both testaments and a variety of authors is illustrative: 'He has triumphed **gloriously** [by judging]' (Exod. 15:1); 'Your right hand, O LORD, **glorious** in power [by judging]' (Exod. 15:6); 'Who is like you ... awesome in **glorious** deeds [by judging]' (Exod. 15:11); 'He has triumphed **gloriously** [by judging]' (Exod. 15:21); 'Therefore in the East give **glory** to the LORD [because of His judgement]' (Isa. 24:15); 'Give **glory** to the name of the LORD [because of His judgement]' (Isa. 24:15); 'From the ends of the earth we hear songs of praise, of **glory** to the Righteous One [because of His judgement] (Isa. 24:16); 'His **glory** will be before His elders [because of His judgement]' (Isa. 24:23); 'What if God [judges] ... in order to make known the riches of His **glory** for vessels of mercy ...?' (Rom. 9:23); 'Fear God and give Him **glory** because the hour of His judgement has come' (Rev. 14:7); '**Glory** and power belong to our God, for His judgements are true and just, for He has judged the great prostitute ...' (Rev. 19:1).

† Rom. 9:17, 22; Exod. 15:6.

‡ Exod. 15:6, 7.

§ Exod. 15:7.

¶ Exod. 15:11; Isa. 24:23.

** Exod. 15:11.

†† Rom. 9:20, 21.

‡‡ Rom. 9:22.

§§ Rom. 9:23.

¶¶ Isa. 24:14; Exod. 15:7.

*** Isa. 24:16.

††† Isa. 26:21.

can grasp the greatness of His glory is the extent to which we can endure the loss of an unbeliever. The degree to which we prize His glory is the degree to which we will cope. The more we can align ourselves with God by having His glory as the grid through which we see and evaluate everything, the more we'll be able to process and live with His judgement of rebels we loved.

Part of God's Greatness is His Goodness

Part of God's glory is His unfailing goodness to His people, whether or not we are able to understand it. A testimony I read recently bears out the power of being committed to this truth:

> In 1987, someone brutally murdered my brother. He was almost thirty-two years old. Just three months earlier, I shared the message of Christ and how he could be born again. He said to me on that day, 'I can't. I have some things to do.' My heart sank as the door of his heart closed. I don't know everything that happened to him between me sharing the gospel and his appointment with death. I want to think he was born again, but I know I can't play mental games here by wishing him into heaven. He may or may not be a Christian. When I arrive in heaven, I will look for my brother. In the meantime, I know these two things: God is good today. God will be good in the future.*

Wonderfully, we never have to choose between worshiping God's glory or enjoying His goodness. The latter is part of the former. His goodness is for the sake of His glory. Psalm 23 opens with a magnificent run-down of God's goodness: He is our loving shepherd; because of Him we are not in want; He makes us lie down in green pastures; He leads us beside quiet waters; He restores our souls; He leads us in paths of righteousness. But why does He do all these things for us? The climax of the

---

* Rick Thomas, https://lifeovercoffee.com/five-things-to-know-when-unbelievers-who-die/ Accessed 17 May, 2023.

catalogue is the reason: He is good to us in all these ways *'for His name's sake.'* For His glory. We magnify His glory when we enjoy His goodness.

Yet as we've already seen, God's glory is also wonderfully wider and deeper than simply His goodness. It has other dimensions as well. And so, for all that has been said in this book until now, the bottom line of being able to live with the loss of an apparent unbeliever is this: having a God whose glory matters more to us than anything else in the universe. We need to see God as He is: truly awesome – in the true, original sense of the word. We need to cultivate a joyful, awe-struck fear of Him. We need to be mentally on our faces before Him. (And why not physically, in our personal devotional times?) We need to be centred on Him rather than ourselves or anyone else. I have sought intentionally to make this a God-centred book, hence the chapter headings. God-centredness is our only hope. It is our greatest hope not only in the tragedy which is the theme of this book, but in every tragedy. And the greater the tragedy, the more this is the case. Here are some Bible characters to show us this by their example.

Job

Job experiences appalling suffering of many kinds. It even includes the sudden, violent deaths of his children – children whose spiritual standing before God had worried him.[†] God's answer to Job's suffering isn't simply to reverse it, although He does do that in the final verses of the book.[‡] Before that reversal, God's answer is to spread before Job a four-chapter vision of His

---

* Ps. 23:1–3.

† Job 1:5.

‡ Job 42:10–17.

glory as lengthy and magnificent as any in Scripture.* And it is God's glory to which Job clings in the immediate aftermath of his suffering at the start of the book:

> Then Job arose and tore his robe and shaved his head and fell on the ground *and worshiped* [that is, he acknowledged God's glory]. And he said ... 'The LORD gave and the LORD has taken away; *blessed be the name of the LORD* [that is, may the LORD be glorified].'

Job is able to accept God's will, even when it is agonising, even when it seems to make no sense to Job, on the basis of who God is and what God is like – His glory.

Eli

Job might have had concerns about his children's standing before the Lord; Eli could have no doubts. Eli's sons were consistently, defiantly, blasphemously wicked, and God was devastatingly clear about their judgement: 'The two ears of everyone who hears it will tingle.'† Eli's response? 'He is the LORD [a reference to God's nature and character – the essence of His glory] – let Him do what is good in His eyes.'‡ Eli isn't being sarcastic or apathetic or fatalistic. He's doing exactly what Job did earlier: managing to accept the will of God because it manifests the character of God – in other words, the glory of God.

Paul

Back in Chapter 1, we saw the anguish of Elijah and Jeremiah and Paul at the eternal loss of those they cared about. Here's the striking thing: in each of those passages, all three individuals

---

* Job 38–41.
† 1 Sam. 3:11.
‡ 1 Sam. 3:18.

cling to the same thing for solace: the display of God's character – that is, His glory. For example, listen to Paul at the start of Romans 9. How does he cope with the prospect of his kinsmen heading for judgement? 'Is there injustice on God's part [for choosing to judge certain people]?' he asks later in Romans 9. 'By no means! For He says to Moses, "I will have mercy on whom I have mercy, and I will have compassion on whom I have compassion."'* The words Paul quotes there from Exodus 33:19 are God's answer to Moses' request in the previous verse, Exodus 33:18, 'Please show me *your glory*'!†

And Paul then continues with this same logic, that the demonstration of God's nature (in other words, His glory) is the justifying purpose behind God's judgement: 'For the Scripture says to Pharaoh, "For this very purpose I have raised you up [for judgement], that I might *show my power* in you, and that *my name might be proclaimed* in all the earth."'‡ And a couple of verses later: 'What if God, desiring to *show his wrath* and to *make known his power*, has endured with much patience vessels of wrath prepared for destruction in order to *make known the riches of his glory* for vessels of mercy ...?'§

In Summary

God's glory is the ultimate reality upon which to stand if we are to endure any other reality. So the question is whether our ability to see and admire aspects of His character shining out of all circumstances – even the darkest – is sufficient to overcome our tragedies. If not, we risk being overcome *by* those tragedies. Will my love for God's glory be sufficient to eclipse

---

* Rom. 9:14, 15.

† Exod. 33:18.

‡ Rom. 9:17.

§ Rom. 9:22, 23.

my struggles? If not, I run the danger of being eclipsed *by* those struggles. The more glorious God is to you, the more He will be a God who anchors your joy and peace and hope, no matter your circumstances. May you walk with a God whose glory matters more to you than anything else in the universe.

7

The God Who Applies

We've covered weighty truths in the preceding pages. But for this book not to have been a waste of your time, those concepts mustn't remain abstract. Our God isn't an impractical academic. Not a single truth in Scripture comes to us without His intention for us to mobilise it in our lives – for us to gain strength and comfort and health by living out its implications. 'Be doers of the word, and not hearers only, deceiving yourselves,' says James.* It was said of Jonathan Edwards that the bulk of his sermons were spent getting his guns into position, and that when he came to apply, that's when he opened fire on the enemy. Satan would love you to sink into a morass of depression and disillusionment over the loss of a loved one. I have tried to be practical throughout, but this chapter especially is when we open fire on him.

1. Pursue Truth.
In his novel *Cloud Cuckoo Land*, Anthony Doerr describes a little girl in medieval times learning to read, and her world expanding exponentially as a result. 'She practices her letters

---

* James 1:22.

on the thousand blank pages of her mind. Each sign signifies a sound, and to link sounds is to form words, and to link words is to construct worlds." Through the tiny, innumerable building blocks of our thoughts, each of us is constantly constructing the worlds we inhabit. Use this book to think intentionally and scripturally around the difficult subject of God's judgement. In your pain, don't shy away from substantive theology. Make God's thoughts your thoughts. Build your world carefully. Paul urges, 'Whatever is true ... think about such things.'† And you will find, as C. S. Lewis promised (in the Introduction), that truth leads to comfort.

2. Draw Near to God

In Chapter 1, we saw the depth and passion of God's care for you. As much as you might want to withdraw from Him in the aftermath of your loss, now is the time to do the opposite. Through prayer and Scripture and fellowship, lean into Him. Do this as a discipline, whether you feel like it or not. God-willing, your heart will follow. '*Come to me*, all who labor and are heavy laden', Jesus urges, 'and I will give you rest. Take my yoke upon you, and learn from me, for I am gentle and lowly in heart, and you will find rest for your souls.'‡ Now is the time to run towards the One who understands your grief more than anyone, the Man of Sorrows Himself,§ the One who treasures your tears, uses them for good, and will one day wipe them away forever.

---

* Anthony Doerr, *Cloud Cuckoo Land* (Scribner, 2021), 45.
† Phil. 4:8.
‡ Matt. 11:28, 29. In context, Jesus' words here are evangelistic, but the principle can be extended.
§ Isa. 53:3.

3. Grieve Well

A stiff upper lip is more British than biblical, more stoical than Scriptural. Of course it is right to be courageous and resilient and to trust God. But these are not mutually exclusive with healthy, natural, God-honouring grief. As we examined in chapter two, we have a God who not only understands our sorrow but shares it. Follow the example of Scripture's unashamed, articulate, godly grievers – people like Job, and Jeremiah in Lamentations, and David in the Psalms. Use their words to give voice to your own grief.

4. Share God's Comfort to You with Others

In 2 Corinthians 1, Paul blesses 'the Father of mercies and God of all comfort, who comforts us in all our affliction *so that we may be able to comfort those who are in any affliction with the comfort with which we ourselves are comforted.*'* He continues, 'If we are afflicted, *it is for your comfort ...*'† There are many brothers and sisters around you aching with your same ache. Come alongside them with the truths we've looked at. Make your grief productive. Let it bear fruit. Don't waste it.

5. Cultivate Contentment in Your Incomplete Knowledge

As we saw in Chapter 3, God alone has the ability and the right to know a person's heart at their point of death. Know that there will be surprises in heaven. Trust your Father's wisdom in giving you as much or as little indication of another's eternity as He has deemed best for you. Don't seek to peer beyond the evidence He has chosen to put before you. Don't look for signs in dreams or other cryptic indications. You will likely end up experiencing wish-fulfilment, as well as weakening your faith

---

* 2 Cor. 1:3, 4.

† 2 Cor. 1:6.

in the sufficiency of God's Word. Accept that 'For now, we see in a mirror dimly.'*

6. Learn to Leave People With the Lord

Consciously work and pray at entrusting people to your Heavenly Father. As we've explored throughout this book, He is good and wise and just far beyond our current understanding. You can trust Him with your loved one's future. The more you are able to leave people with the Lord, the more you will find relief and peace. Let God be God.

7. Be Serious about Your Own Salvation

In Luke 13, Jesus cites tragedies in which Galileans were murdered by Romans and others died in a natural disaster when the tower of Siloam collapsed. His sobering point to his listeners is that 'unless you repent, you will all likewise perish.'†
In Chapter 4, we considered the God who judges. He intends this loss of others to drive us to confirm that we really *have* escaped the wrath to come. Paul reminds the Corinthians 'of the gospel ... by which you are being saved, if you hold fast to the word I preached to you – unless you believed in vain.'‡
He's challenging them to check that they really *are* holding onto the word of life, that they really *are* believing. Paul warns the Philippians to 'work out your own salvation with fear and trembling'§ – that is, to pursue it urgently rather than presume on it complacently.

It is possible to be unhealthily introspective, at the cost of God-honouring assurance. But it is also possible to be casual

---

* 1 Cor. 13:12.

† Luke 13:3, 5.

‡ 1 Cor 15:1, 2.

§ Phil. 2:12.

and complacent and presumptuous. God uses the loss of others to warn us away from this. Pause right now. Visualise standing before God in a few hours' time. (You just might be. In Puritan Arthur Dent's words, 'We should always live as if we should die, or that our bed should be our grave; [we] must live continually as if Christ should come to judgment presently.'*) As you read these words, are you really repenting of your sin? Are you really trusting in Christ's death alone as the grounds for God to accept you? 'We are but a heartbeat from eternity, which hangs upon the thin thread of time ... Our lives are not just a journey to death; we are journeying to heaven, that eternal day that knows no sunset, or to hell, the eternal night which knows no sunrise.'† Journey carefully. Journey deliberately.

8. Put Sin to Death

Part of being serious about our salvation is being ruthless about our sin. In Matthew's Gospel, Jesus teaches, 'If your right eye causes you to sin, tear it out and throw it away. *For it is better that you lose one of your members than that your whole body be thrown into hell.* And if your right hand causes you to sin, cut it off and throw it away. *For it is better that you lose one of your members than that your whole body go into hell.*'‡ Christ unashamedly uses the horror of hell to drive home the seriousness of sin, for hell is where sin leads in the end. We are saved not by our fight against sin, but by faith. Yet if our faith is real, it will manifest itself in a desperate fight against sin. What do you need to repent of right now? What practical steps do

---

* Arthur Dent, *The Plain Man's Pathway to Heaven; Wherein Every Man May Clearly See Whether He Shall Be Saved or Damned* (1599; repr., Soli Deo Gloria, 1994), 1.

† Joel R. Beeke and Mark Jones, A *Puritan Theology: Doctrine for Life* (Reformation Heritage Books, 2012), 856.

‡ Matt. 5:29, 30.

you need to take, no matter how extreme, to 'tear out' and 'cut off' sin from your life?

9. Be Humbled by Your Own Salvation

Someone who fears for the salvation of loved ones emailed me with the following words: 'The death of unbelieving loved ones is an occasion for believers to express earnest worship and profound gratitude to God ... They should bow their heads with humility, knowing it is only by God's electing grace that they themselves know him as savior.' None of us have any right to salvation. The arresting truth isn't that some aren't saved – it's that any *are*. The tragedy of the loss of others throws into relief the miracle of our own escape. We should be gasping, 'There but for the grace of God go I.' The psalmist knew this: 'I give thanks to you, O Lord my God, with my whole heart, and I will glorify your name forever. For great is your steadfast love toward me; you have delivered my soul from the depths of Sheol.'*

10. Be Urgent in Evangelism

A friend of mine once told me of a dream he'd had, of watching an endless line of people shuffling through a doorway into flames beyond. One of them suddenly turned to face him. He realised with a start that this was his own non-Christian roommate. The roommate said, 'Why didn't you tell me about this?' Then he woke with a start. Allow your loss to fuel your evangelism, and may God use that to prevent the loss of others. Take up the judgement-tinged urgency at the end of Psalm 2, 'Kiss the Son, lest He be angry, and you perish in the way, for His wrath is quickly kindled. Blessed are all who take refuge in Him.'†

---

* Ps. 86:12, 13.

† Ps. 2:12.

11. Don't Bear Responsibility for the Lost which isn't Ultimately Yours

In the final analysis, lost people never end up in hell because of our failure to witness to them or pray for them. As we saw in Chapter 4, they end up in hell because of their willful determination to reject God, and because of His mysterious sovereign choice. Don't assume a burden of responsibility which isn't ultimately yours, and which you will not be able to bear. Repent of the inevitable failures to witness and pray which we all have, receive God's forgiveness and grace, and acknowledge that His perfect will is inexorable. Don't bear responsibility for the lost which isn't finally yours.

12. Be Quick to Forgive Unbelievers

'Beloved, never avenge yourselves, but leave it to the wrath of God, for it is written, "Vengeance is mine, I will repay, says the Lord."'* God's vengeance on an unbeliever will be far more severe than yours could ever be. Perhaps they have wronged you horrifically. Consider hell, then see if you are still able to aim bitter resentment at them. Your tears will shortly be wiped away, and unless something changes, they will shortly enter terrible suffering forever. Extend forgiveness to them. You will be obeying God, doing good to yourself, and witnessing to them.

13. Be Receptive to Refinement

In Chapter 5, we saw that God is using your tragedy for your refinement, and we considered examples of what this might look like. Be open to God lovingly, painfully doing that work in your life. We can be quick to jump on the promise of Romans 8:28, that God works all things together for good for His people. But we are not always as quick to define what 'good' is – which the

---

* Rom. 12:19.

very next verse does: it is 'to be conformed to the image of His Son.'* Consider the goldsmith who purifies gold by turning up the heat. As the gold melts, impurities float to the surface and are skimmed off. How does he know when he has completed the process? When he can see his own reflection in the precious metal. Know that God is using the awfulness of your loss to make you more like Christ. Ponder how He might be doing this so that you can be leaning into that process.

14. Keep the Eternal Perspective

In the graveyard of a church in Dundee lies an ancient, weathered stone, blank except for one word engraved in large letters: 'Eternity'. One of the church's pastors (perhaps the great Robert Murray M'Cheyne in the 1800s) had wanted people to consider the coming 'forever' on their way in and out of church.† As we saw in Chapter 5, the reality of eternity changes everything. The next world is when we will finally perceive God's judgement with perfected hearts and minds, finally see the true horror of sin, finally value His glory as it deserves, finally have every tear wiped away, finally be able to rejoice and be at peace. As Paul promises the Corinthians, 'Now we know in part; then we shall know fully.'‡

15. Keep Your Loves Well-Ordered.

Augustine of Hippo helpfully explained sin in terms of wrongly-ordered loves. He showed that we are prone to loving less important things more, and more important things less. The first of the Ten Commandments, for example, is effectively

---

* Rom. 8:29.

† Joel R. Beeke and Mark Jones, A *Puritan Theology: Doctrine for Life* (Reformation Heritage Books, 2012), 857.

‡ 1 Cor. 13:12.

to have no other loves before our love for God.* Jesus likewise taught that the most important commandment is to love God, and the second is to love my neighbour.† When I reverse the order of these, I place a greater weight of love and worship on lesser objects than is appropriate, and a lesser weight of love and worship on the greater object then He deserves.

Cultivate a love for God and His glory which outshines your love for anyone else. Resist idolising any other person over Him. This, ironically, is what will enable you to love any other person *better*. The best thing I can do for my wife and children is to love God more than them – that's what will enable me to be a better husband and father. The best thing I can do for my unsaved loved ones is to love God more than them – that's what will enable me to be a better, kinder person around them and a better witness to them. On top of this, keeping God first will enable you to survive the eternal loss of any other person. Otherwise, if they are first, and perish, it will be your god who has perished, leaving you to unravel.

16. Treasure Christ

On the cross, Jesus bore the righteous wrath of God for the sin of His people. He was enduring hell itself. In fact, He was experiencing the equivalent of all the eternities in hell that all of His millions of people would have faced. This depth of suffering is unfathomable. Yet it is what Jesus went through for you! This is how much He loves you! And in His ability to be that sinless substitute for you, here is His perfect purity, precious and beautiful beyond description. In the hell of the cross, here is His courage, His selflessness, His faithfulness. The magnificence of Christ blazes out of the darkness of the doctrine of hell.

---

* Exod. 20:3.
† Matt. 22:36–40.

He is a Christ whose value and splendour will light up your life, regardless of your circumstances. Treasure Him.

In the End

In the end, my one final word of encouragement and hope is simply this: 'Let us fix our eyes on Jesus, the author and perfecter of our faith ...'* Jesus Christ exemplified perfectly for us the applications of this chapter. When we fail at them, as we will, it is Jesus Christ whose blood has paid for those failures, and whose grace enables us to pick ourselves up, dust ourselves down, and try again. And it is Jesus Christ Himself who is at the heart of each one:

He is the truth; the One to whom we draw near in our loss; the One to whom we take our grief; the One to whom we point those we're comforting; the One in whom we rest with our incomplete knowledge of the fates of others; the One on whom we focus when checking our own salvation; the One whose urgent warnings we heed when we put sin to death; the One before whom we bow in relief and humble thanks as we consider our own miraculous escape from the wrath to come; the One to whom we point others as we witness; the One who has atoned for our failures to witness and who cleanses our consciences by the cross; the One whose example teaches us to forgive others; the One who will be at the centre of the coming eternity when everything becomes clear; the One of infinite value, whose glory now and forever is worthy of our highest love and commitment.

Fix your eyes on Him.

---

* Heb. 12:2 (NIV).

Scripture Index

Subject Index

Another book by Will Dobbie

From Everlasting to Everlasting
Every Believer's Biography
Will Dobbie

- 30-day short daily readings
- Explains Ordo Salutis
- For laypeople

This devotional walks readers through the stage-by-stage path of God's salvation, from eternity past, through life and death, and into eternity future. The book explores rich, substantive theology, making it accessible and clear without dumbing it down, and includes illustrations and applications. The stages of the Ordo Salutis as Will Dobbie frames it are spread across thirty daily devotionals. Life in our world can include uncertainty, anxiety and tragedy. In this context, the theological richness and profundity of God's salvation plan offers the believer confidence, comfort, clarity and perspective, to God's greater glory.

ISBN: 978-1-5271-0837-0

Christian Focus Publications

Our mission statement –

STAYING FAITHFUL

In dependence upon God we seek to impact the world through literature faithful to His infallible Word, the Bible. Our aim is to ensure that the Lord Jesus Christ is presented as the only hope to obtain forgiveness of sin, live a useful life and look forward to heaven with Him.

Our books are published in four imprints:

CHRISTIAN
FOCUS

Popular works including biographies, commentaries, basic doctrine and Christian living.

CHRISTIAN
HERITAGE

Books representing some of the best material from the rich heritage of the church.

MENTOR

Books written at a level suitable for Bible College and seminary students, pastors, and other serious readers. The imprint includes commentaries, doctrinal studies, examination of current issues and church history.

CF4•K

Children's books for quality Bible teaching and for all age groups: Sunday school curriculum, puzzle and activity books; personal and family devotional titles, biographies and inspirational stories – because you are never too young to know Jesus!

Christian Focus Publications Ltd,
Geanies House, Fearn, Ross-shire,
IV20 1TW, Scotland, United Kingdom.